Tropical Teasers

by Lisa Vogt

Construction of Projects: Lori Soles, Joe & Lisa Vogt

Photography: Joe & Lisa Vogt

FIRST EDITION: *Published in the United States*

DISTRIBUTION: *Stained Glass Images Inc.*

ISBN: 0936459-44-1

© *1999 - Lisa Vogt*

All rights reserved. No part of this publication may be reproduced, stored in a retrieval system, or transmitted in any form or by any means, electronic, mechanical, photocopying, recording or otherwise, without the prior permission of the copyright owner, with the exception of pattern reproduction for personal use in constructing the projects.

Our books, patterns and other fine products are available from stained glass suppliers everywhere! For a catalog, please contact:

STAINED GLASS IMAGES INC.
135 Dolton Ave - San Carlos, CA. 94070
(650) 592-4858 or 1-800-782-4645
e-mail: sgimages@ledgernet.com
FAX (650) 592-2890

Peacock

My Secret Garden

Iris and Water Lily

Heron and Pond

Cockatoo & Orchids

Tropical Screen

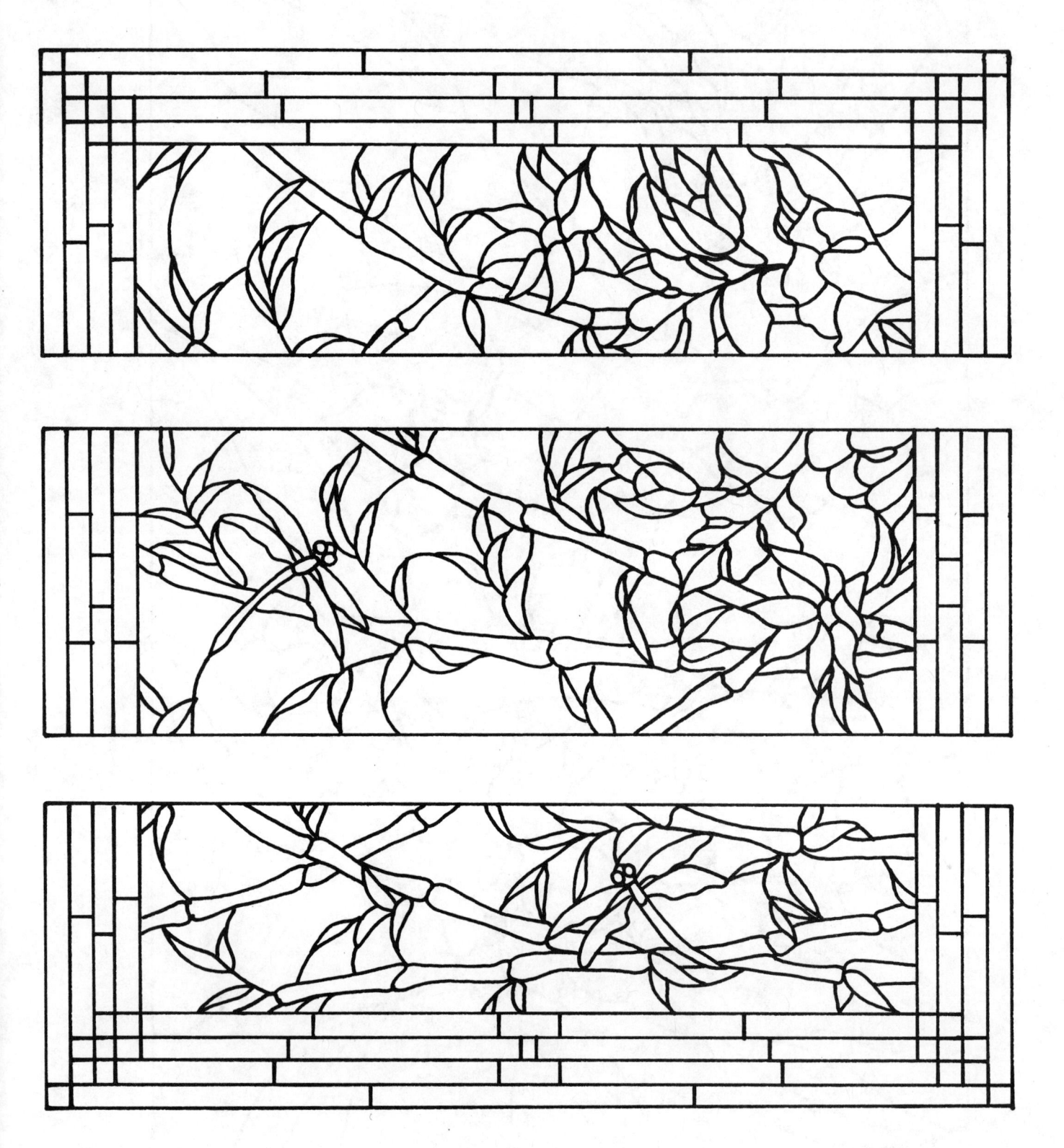

Regatta #2

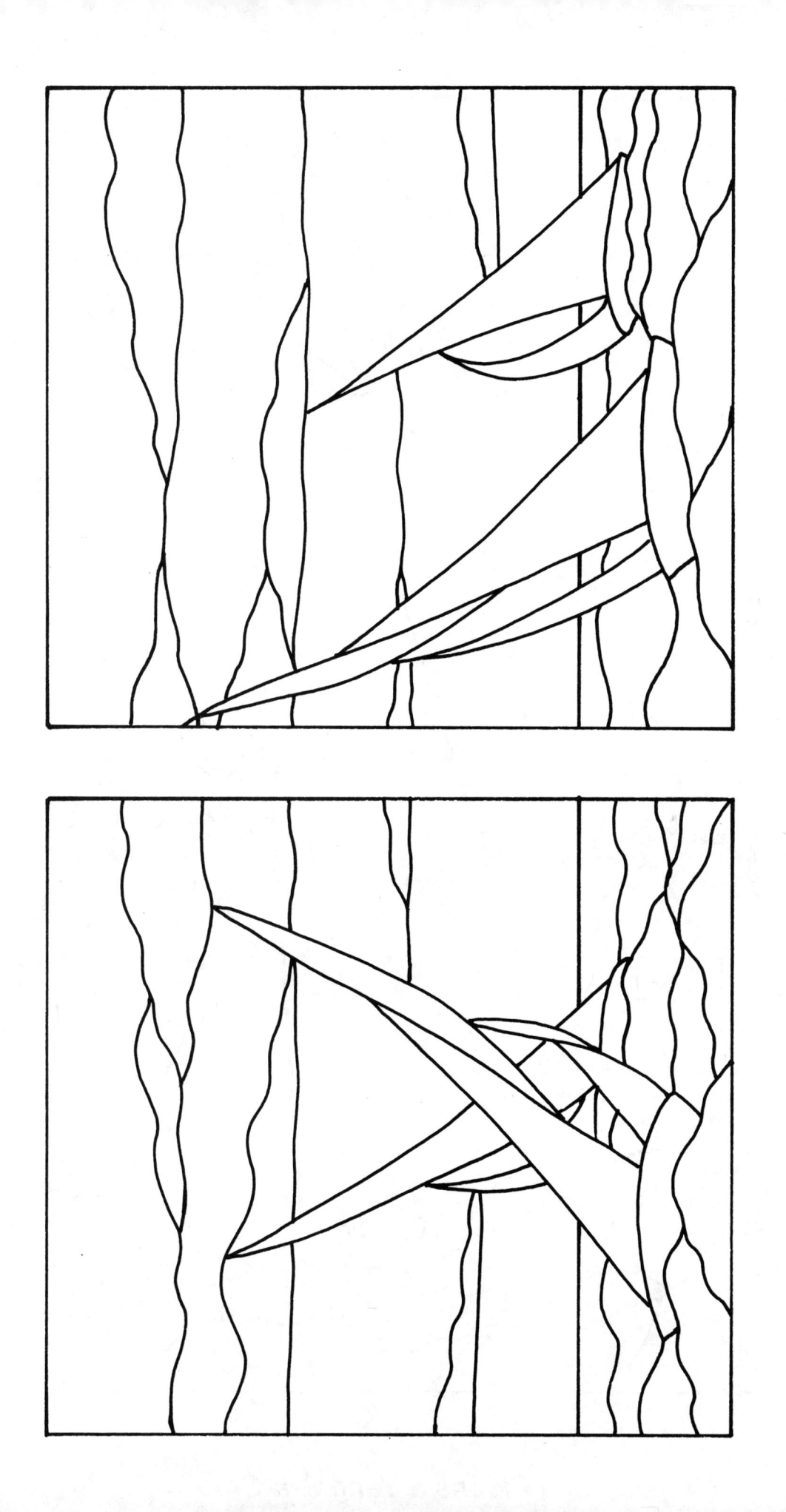

Regatta #1

7

3 Clowns a Tang & a Crab

Coral Reef

Volcano

Mr. Sun

Fancy Feathered Heron

Dolphins

Bird of Paradise Flower

Fantail Fish
(open background)

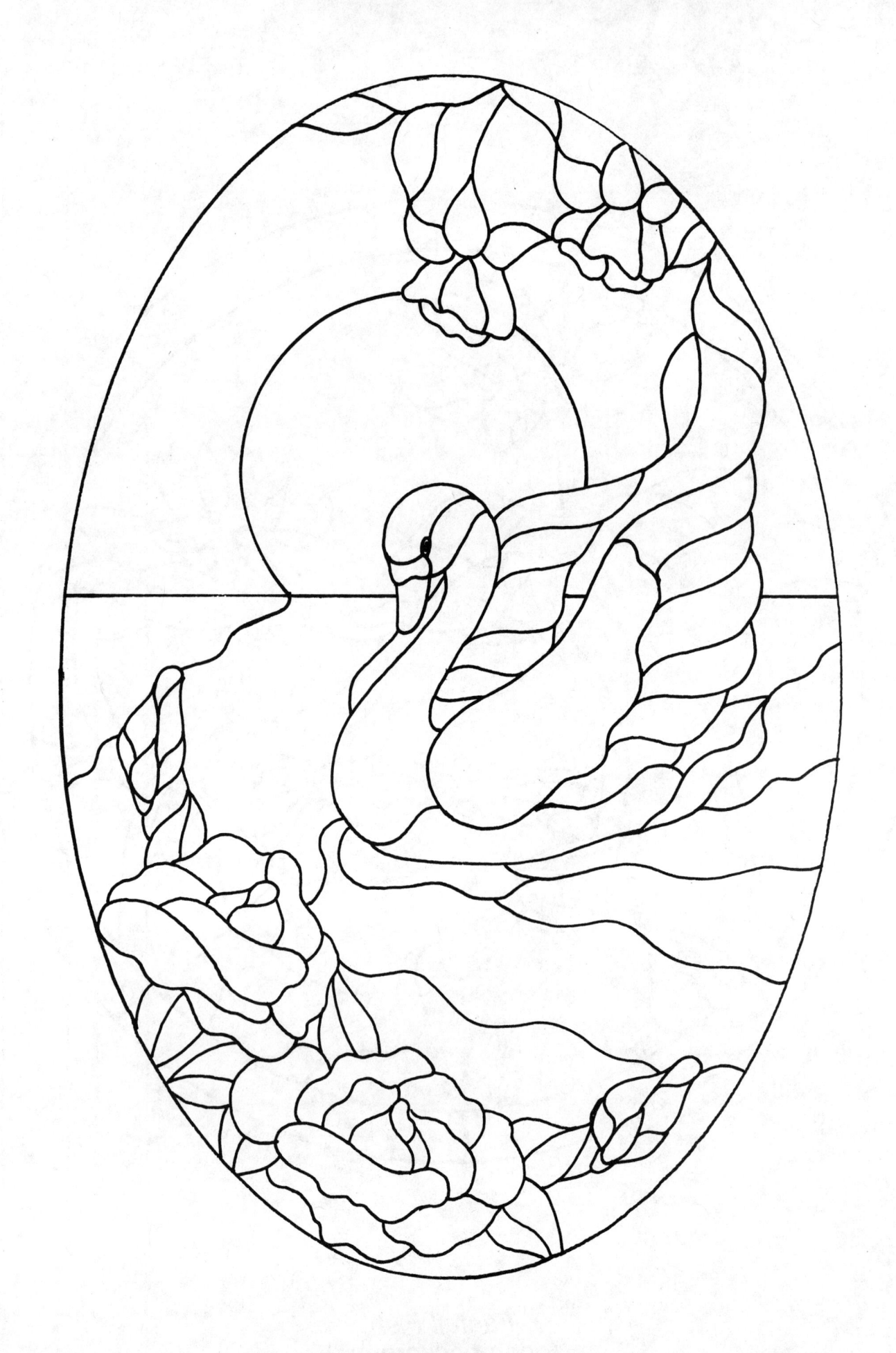

Swan Lake

Iris

Hibiscus Flower

Flamingo Pair

Way Cool Flamingo

Beauty on the Beach

Long Roses

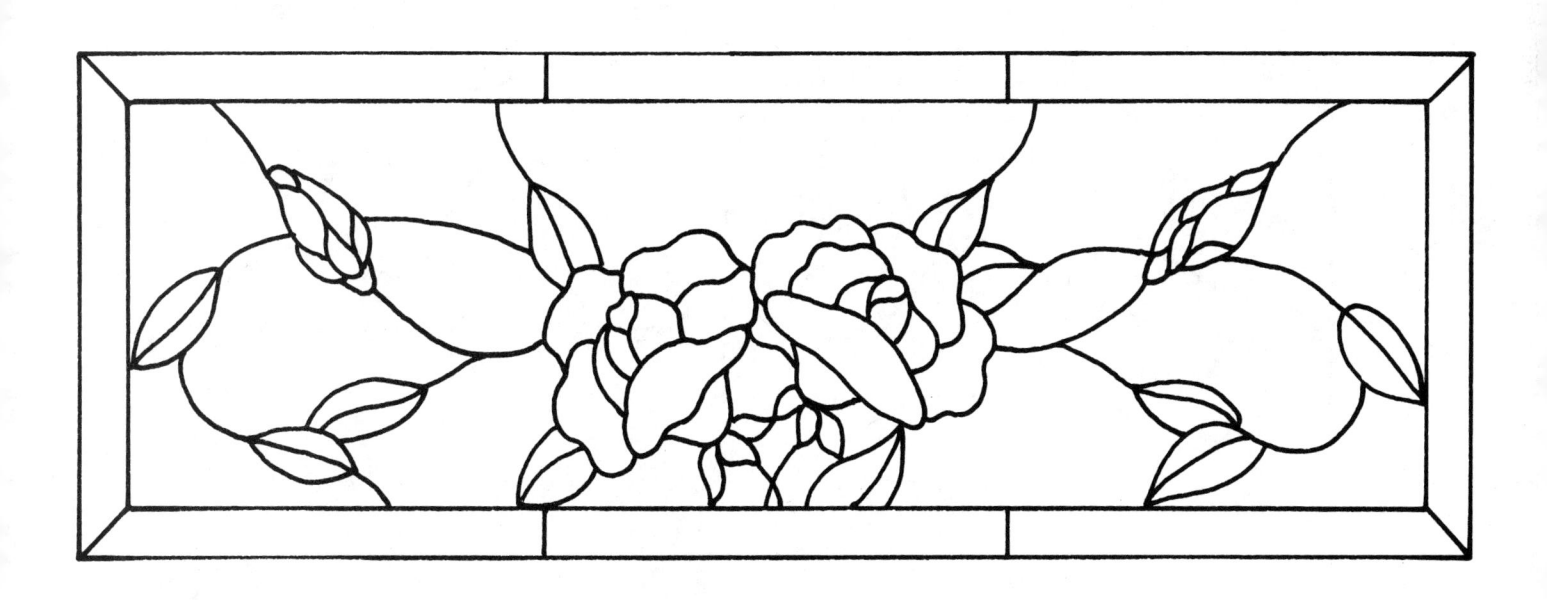

Rose Transom

Sun

Moon

Elegant Lady

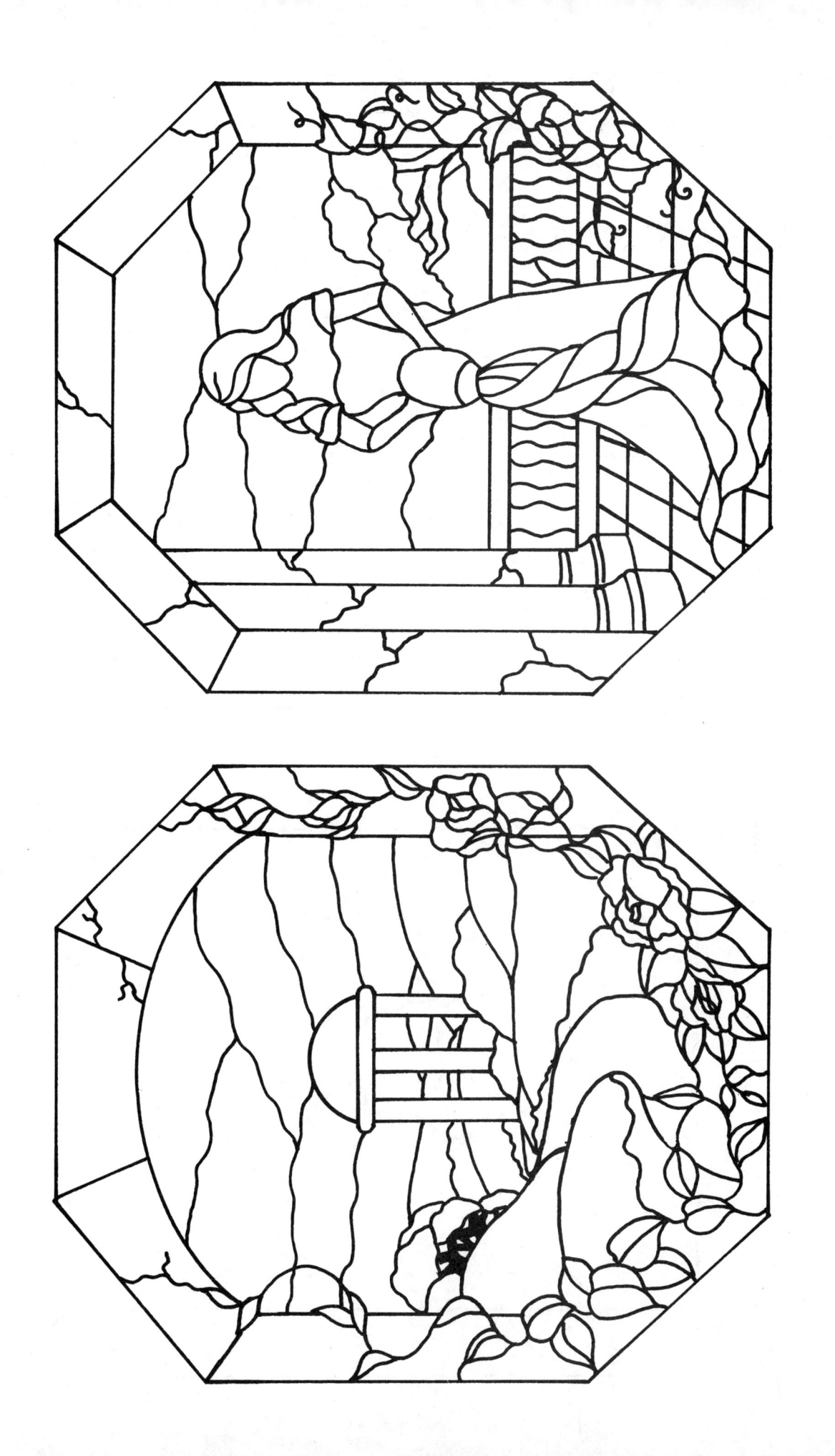

Gazebo

23

Double Orchids

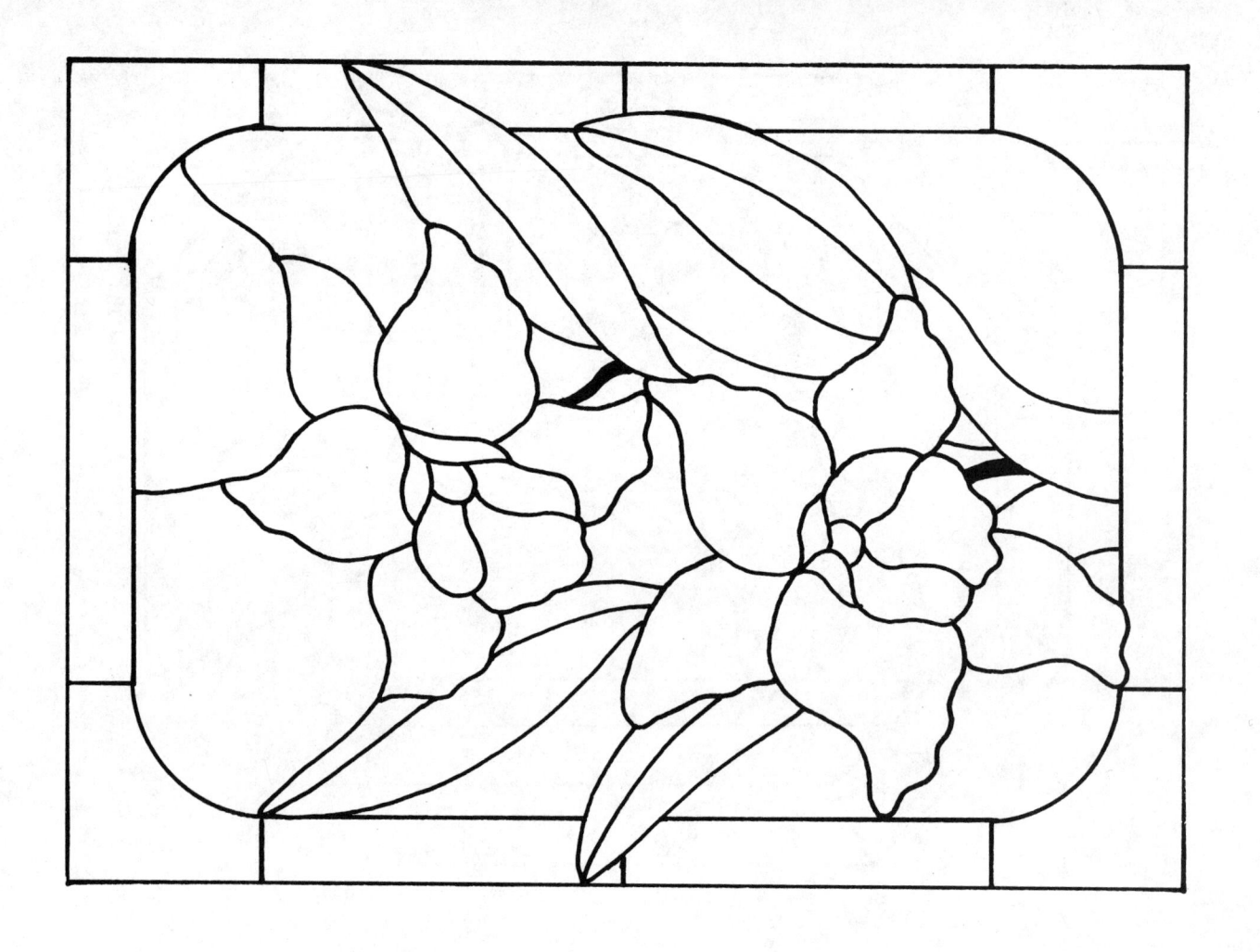

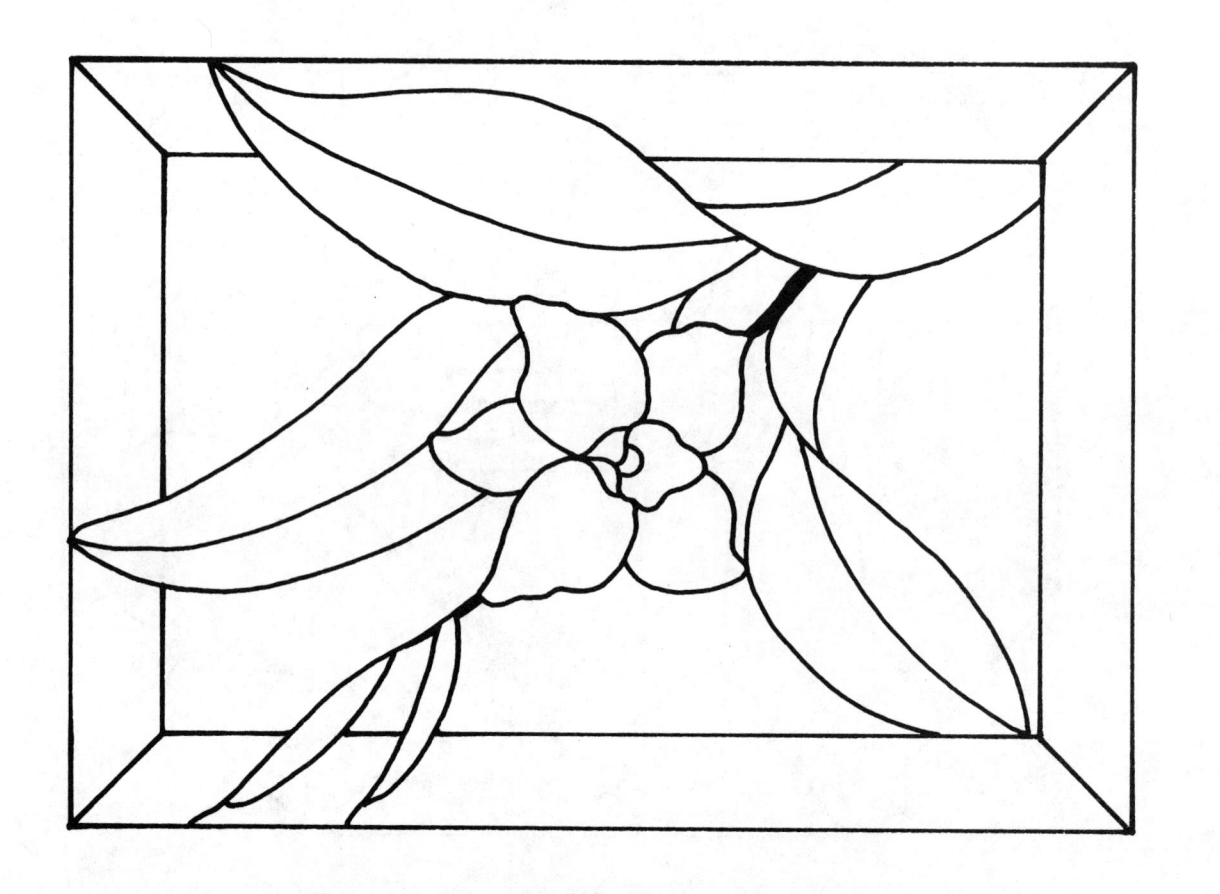

Single Orchid

Sea Shore

Rush Hour

Afternoon Delight #1

26 Afternoon Delight #2

Bird of Paradise Sidelight *Magnolia Sidelight* 27

Vine

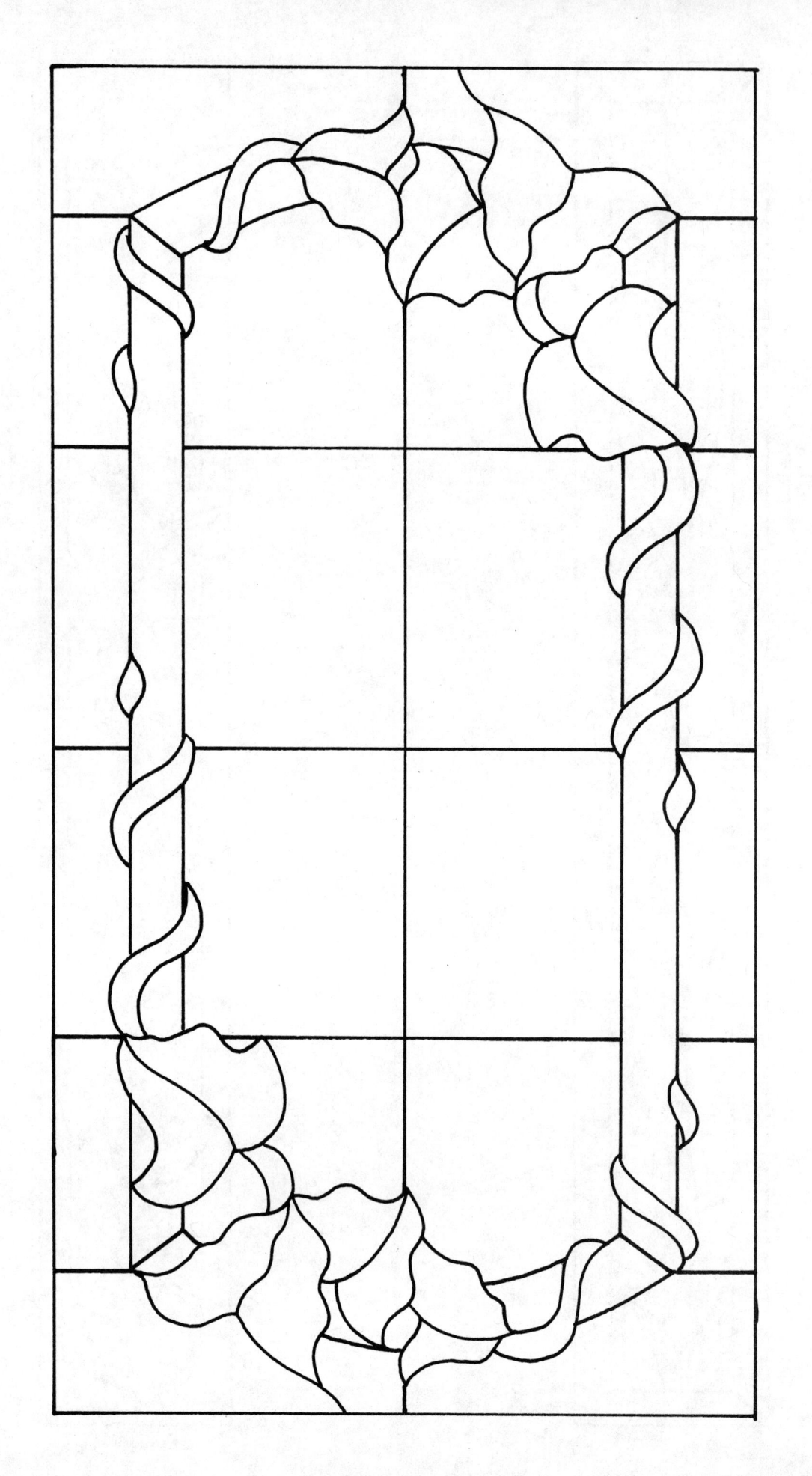

Hummingbird & Fuchsia

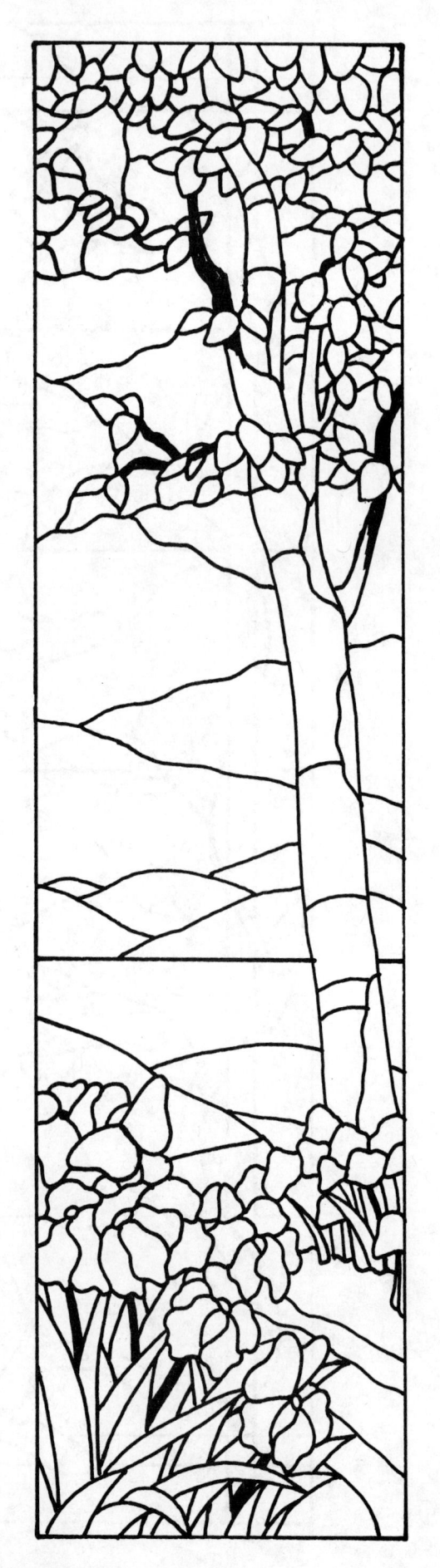

Birches by the Lake

Parrots in Paradise

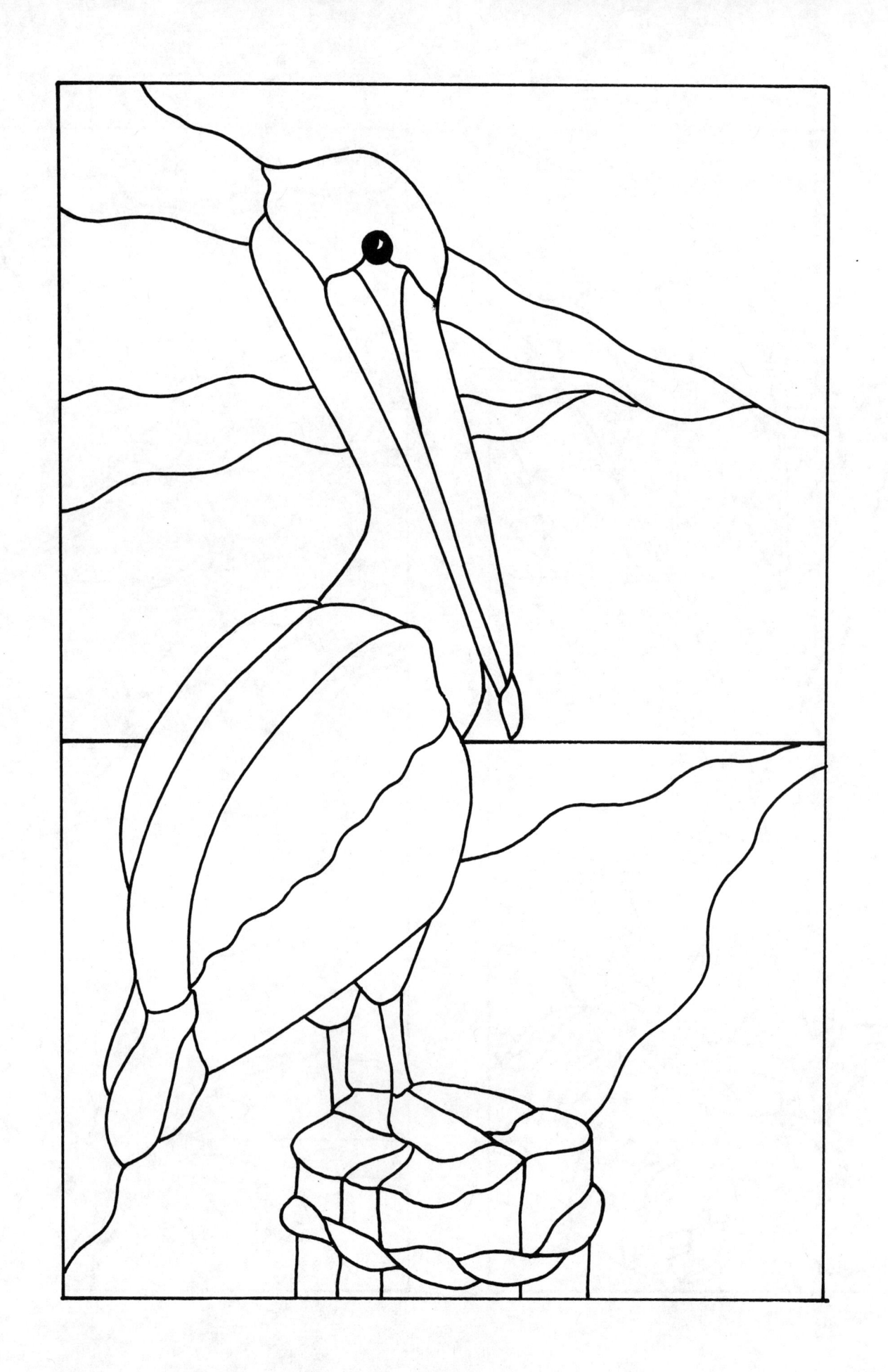

Pelican

Cat in Window

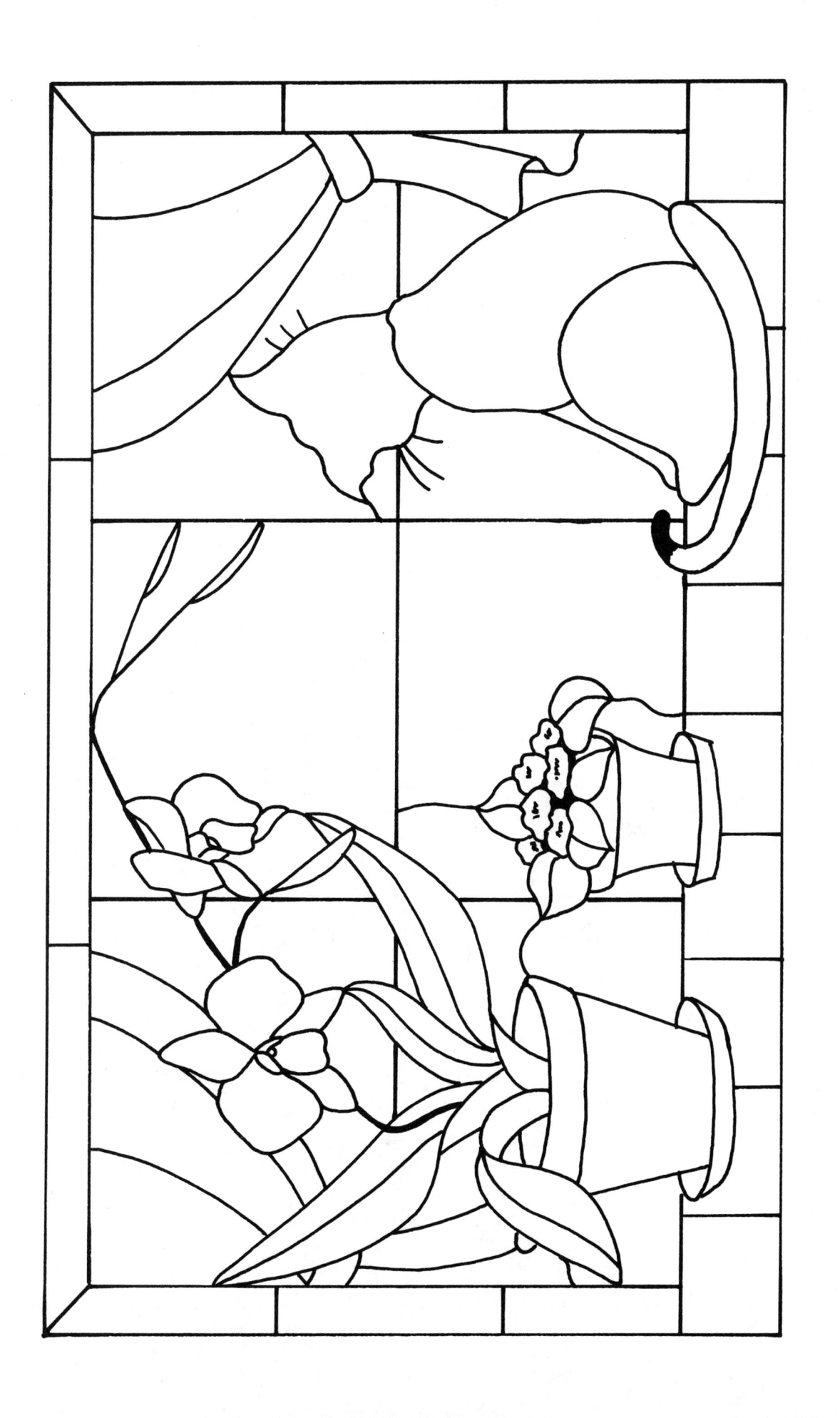

Life's a Beach

Climbing Roses

Sailfish & Flying Fish

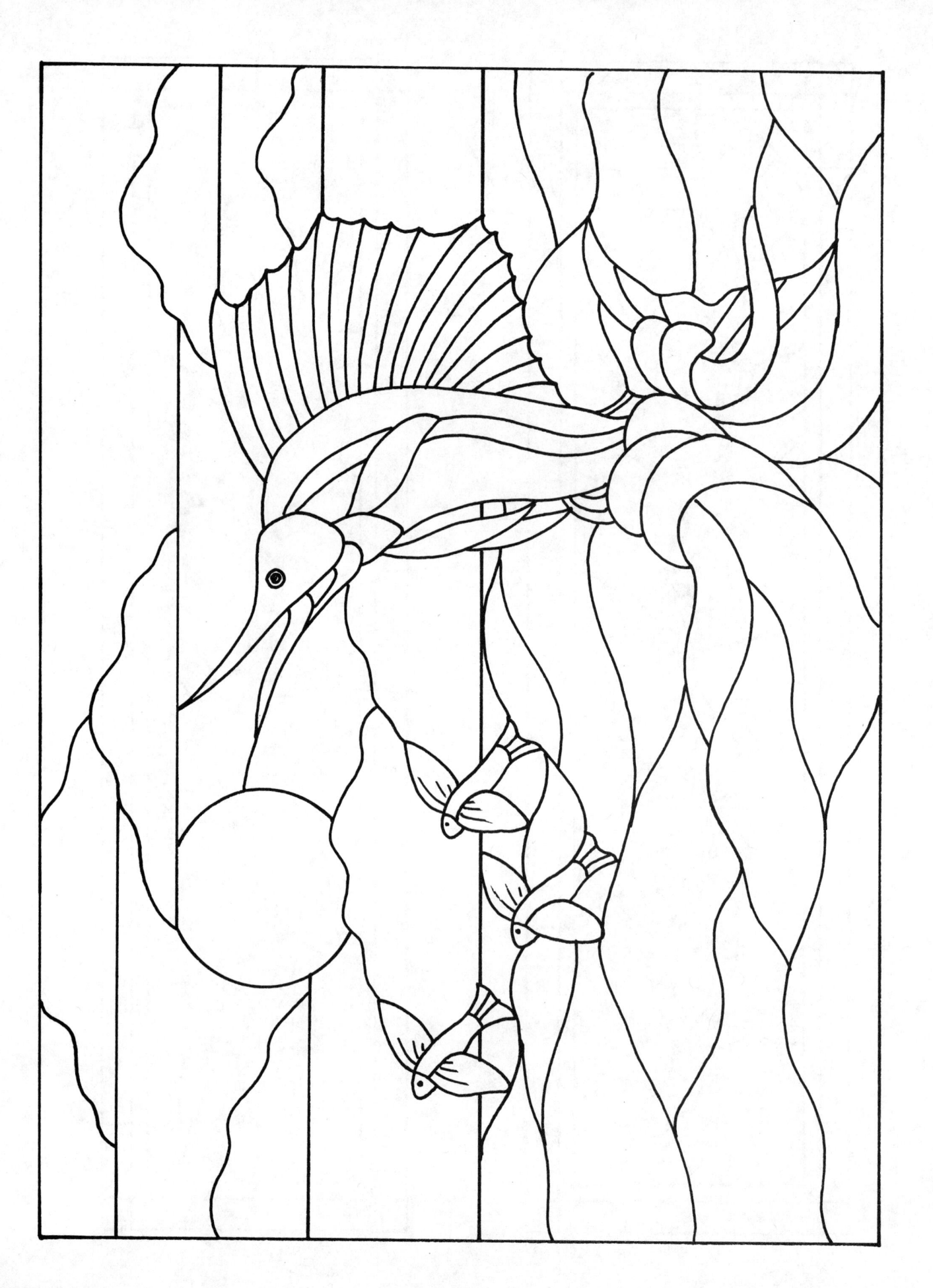

Water Garden

Acknowledgments

As is true with most successful projects, this book was made possible through the efforts of a lot of special people.
I'd like to thank my family for their constant support, thanks to Gene Mayo for saying "Yes", and special thanks to Lori Soles who is a great asset as a co-worker and a good friend.

About the Artist

Lisa Vogt, owner of Originals In Glass, works as a professional stained glass artist in Tampa, Florida. She draws upon her fine art education while designing award winning works of art that have been published in industry publications such as "Stained Glass News" and Carolyn Kyle's "Winning Designs" pattern book. Her work can be found in thousands of residences, churches and professional buildings.